DIXIE

the Rescue Dog
Makes New Friends

ALBUM ONE

Dixie the Rescue Dog
Makes New Friends

ALBUM ONE

ISBN 979-8-9870947-0-9 paperback book
Printed in the USA
Edited by Susan Diamond Riley
Author's interior photo and back cover photo by Izaak Holsapple
Some profile photos were provided courtesy of pet parents.

This book is dedicated to the countless souls
who give their hearts, life, time, and resources to care for
and nurture precious canines in need.

We thank you.

Sheree and Dixie, the Rescue Dog

It wasn't Dixie's first stay at the animal shelter.

The cold cement floor felt sadly familiar, and the wadded-up blanket in the corner wasn't much comfort. The shelter was a nice place, and the volunteers gave Dixie lots of love and attention. But Dixie knew she deserved more. She needed a good home—this time with someone who would take better care of her. The shelter was noisy, with dogs barking and carrying on all day long. But Dixie wasn't the barking kind. Instead, she would sit quietly, wildly wag her tail, and give a look only Dixie could.

One afternoon, a lady came to visit the shelter. She had seen Dixie's picture online and was anxious to meet her.

The lady at the shelter told Mama she thought Dixie was a Pointer mixed with some other kind of dog, but she didn't know for sure.

Dixie's whole body was speckled with a hundred brown, gray, and black spots.

Thick black eyeliner framed her big brown eyes. One side of her face was a caramel color, and the other was white. Even her eyelashes were white on one side and dark on the other. Dixie was so soft that even her ears felt like silk.

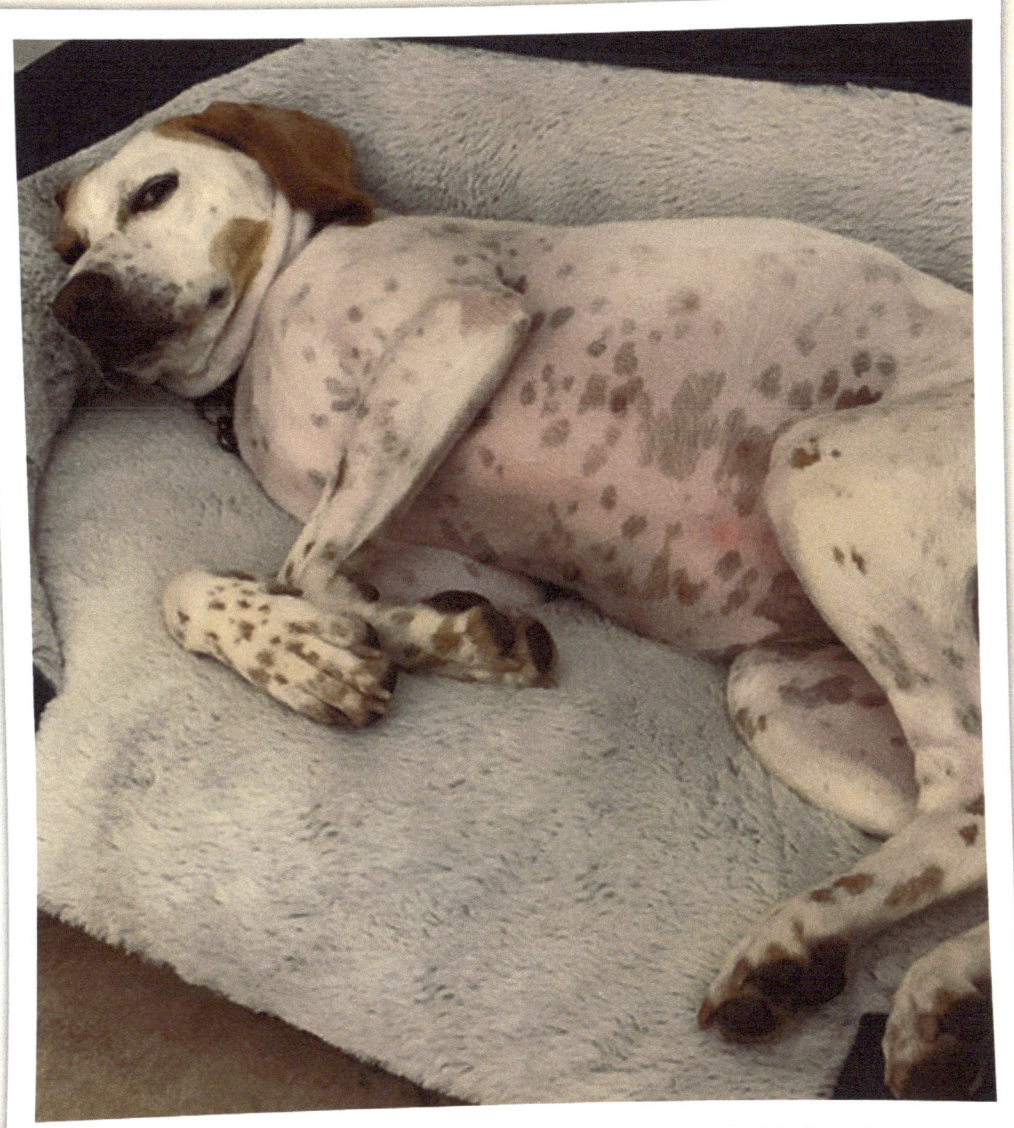

The lady sat on the floor, gave Dixie a big hug, scratched her belly, and kissed her on top of her head.

"You're a sweet little thing." The lady grinned. The sound of her voice made Dixie like her right away.

**"Pick me! Pick me!"
Dixie thought.**

As kind as everyone was at the shelter, she wanted a real home with someone special who would love her—and she could love them right back.

"Hey there, baby girl. How would you like to come home with me?"

It was Dixie's lucky day. Adorned with a brand new collar and matching leash, Dixie excitedly followed the nice lady to her car, hoping this time she was going to her forever home.

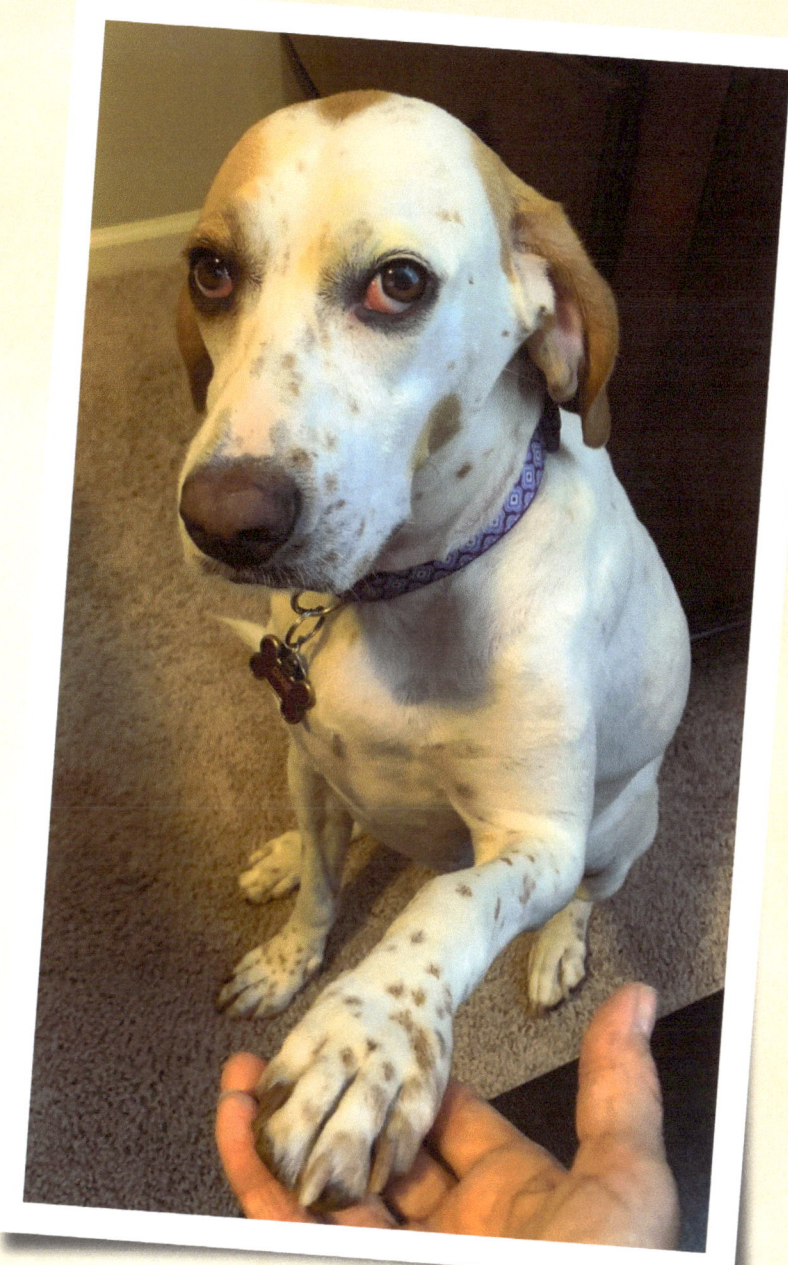

Dixie's new mom bought her a comfy bed, her very own food and water bowls, treats, and stuffed toys.

Her favorite was a big yellow taco. She loved the taco so much that Mama had to keep sewing up all the holes. Dixie's toys were fun to play with, but they were no substitute for real live friends.

It would take a little time for Mama and Dixie to get to know each other, but both of them were hopeful all would go well.

And it did. Dixie loved everything about her new life—especially her new home. There were lots of trees, colorful bushes, and bright orange flowers. It was a big, beautiful, fenced-in yard where she could run, play, and explore.

7

Every day Mama would go out with Dixie to the backyard for playtime.

Dixie would chase the Frisbee, flip it into the air, toss it up again, and then do zoomies around the big pine tree. Mama didn't know where the pup got all that energy, but she loved watching Dixie play.

Dixie was a curious dog.

She was constantly poking her head into the plants, chasing after a lizard or pesky squirrel. Mama loved watching her new puppy dog as she explored every nook and cranny of the yard. When Dixie grew tired of exploring, she would stretch out and lie on the grass in the warm sun. Mama would smile at her playful pup and think how nice it would be for her to have some new friends.

Dixie wasn't the only one new to the neighborhood.

Mama had just moved from far away and didn't know anyone either. Dixie looked up at Mama and thought she looked kind of sad, so she gave her a big kiss on the cheek and laid her head on Mama's lap.

The two of them quickly bonded.

Mama and Dixie spent all their time together playing, learning new tricks, and making homemade dog treats. Of course, Dixie was Mama's official taste tester.

Mama took Dixie for long walks on the beach, to the dog park, and downtown by the waterfront, where they would sit on the wall and watch the boats go by.

Aside from a casual nod from a stranger or a passing "hello," Dixie and Mama hadn't made any new friends in town.

One day while on a walk, Dixie stopped in her tracks when she saw a bright blue plastic rocking horse a neighbor had left out for the trash.

Dixie zeroed in on what she thought was a live animal. She sniffed. She backed up, then lunged forward. But the plastic horse didn't move. It wasn't the kind of friend she was looking for.

Dixie's new yard was alive with lizards, frogs, bugs, and birds.

She tried to make friends with the deer standing in the backyard, but the deer didn't understand. When Dixie would run to greet them, they would leap over the fence and run into the forest. Dixie couldn't figure out why none of them would play with her.

"Dixie!" Mama called.
"Treat! Come inside, sweet girl."

Sometimes the lure of a tasty treat would be enough to get Dixie's attention, and other times she couldn't have cared less. She would stay outside in her yard for hours, hoping to find someone or something fun to play with.

One morning, Mama took Dixie on a walk through the new neighborhood.

To her delight, Dixie saw a group of dogs up ahead! Each one was a different color and size. Dixie had seen plenty of other dogs at the shelter, but never so many out in the open on walks with their pet parents. As she and Mama excitedly headed toward the group, Dixie tugged harder, jumping up and down, nearly pulling Mama over.

"Hello!"

The lady walking the pit bull grinned and introduced herself and her dog, Jack. Jack had only one eye and walked with a slight limp. He cocked his head sideways to look up at Mama and wagged his tail, then happily sniffed Dixie and kissed her on the face.

"Jack is a real gentleman," his mom said. "I adopted him a few years ago. He wouldn't hurt a fly."

"Well, hi there, Jack." Mama petted him on the head.

"He can't hear you either," his mom explained. "He's deaf."

As with most rescued dogs, Dixie and Mama both knew there was a story behind what had happened to Jack and why he was missing an eye and couldn't hear.

Evie, the smallest dog of the group, barked at Dixie and scraped her paws on the ground, flipping dirt and grass all over Dixie's face.

Evie was the toughest one of the bunch and didn't hesitate to throw her weight around, letting the other dogs know who was boss. "Evie, knock it off! Sorry," her dad apologized.

"We call her 'Evil Evie.' She can be a real pill."

"Isn't she a Shih Tzu?" Mama asked.

"Mm hm. And she's also a rescue. Is Dixie, too?"

"Yes. I just moved here and I adopted Dixie right away. We've been hoping to meet some new friends." Dixie happily bounced up and down, tugging and pulling on her leash. Mama rolled her eyes. "As you can see, she has a lot of energy."

Lucy was tugging and pulling, trying to get closer to sniff Dixie—because that's what dogs do.

Lucy and Dixie looked a little bit alike, except Lucy was an all-white Lab-mix. Lucy's pet parents smiled and laughed as the two dogs played and jumped all over each other.

Dixie suddenly stopped playing when she noticed a sleek, chocolate-colored dog named Jarvis.

She had never seen a dog without hair, and neither had Mama.

"Oh my!" Mama cried. "He's beautiful."

Jarvis's mom laughed. "He's a Mexican hairless dog. I adopted him from my veterinarian. He needed an expensive surgery, but his other pet parents couldn't afford it. They asked the vet to find him a good home, and I couldn't resist! I had to have him, surgery and all."

Sure enough, the long walk around the neighborhood proved to be the perfect place to meet new friends.

Brinkley and Baloo were brothers from different mothers.

While Baloo stayed home to guard the house, Brinkley got to go to work with his mom every day. With the passenger window down, he sat majestically next to his mom in the car. He looked absolutely regal—like the mayor in a parade. As they passed by, everyone shouted and waved, "Hi, Brinkley!"

"Well, I think we're all going to become good friends," Evie's mom said with a smile.

"In case you didn't notice, we're a tribe of rescues in this neighborhood. So Dixie will fit in just fine. And so will you."

"If you'd like to join us, we walk every morning," Jack's mom kindly offered. It made Mama's heart swell.

"We would love to. Thank you so much." It wasn't just the dogs who were making new friends.

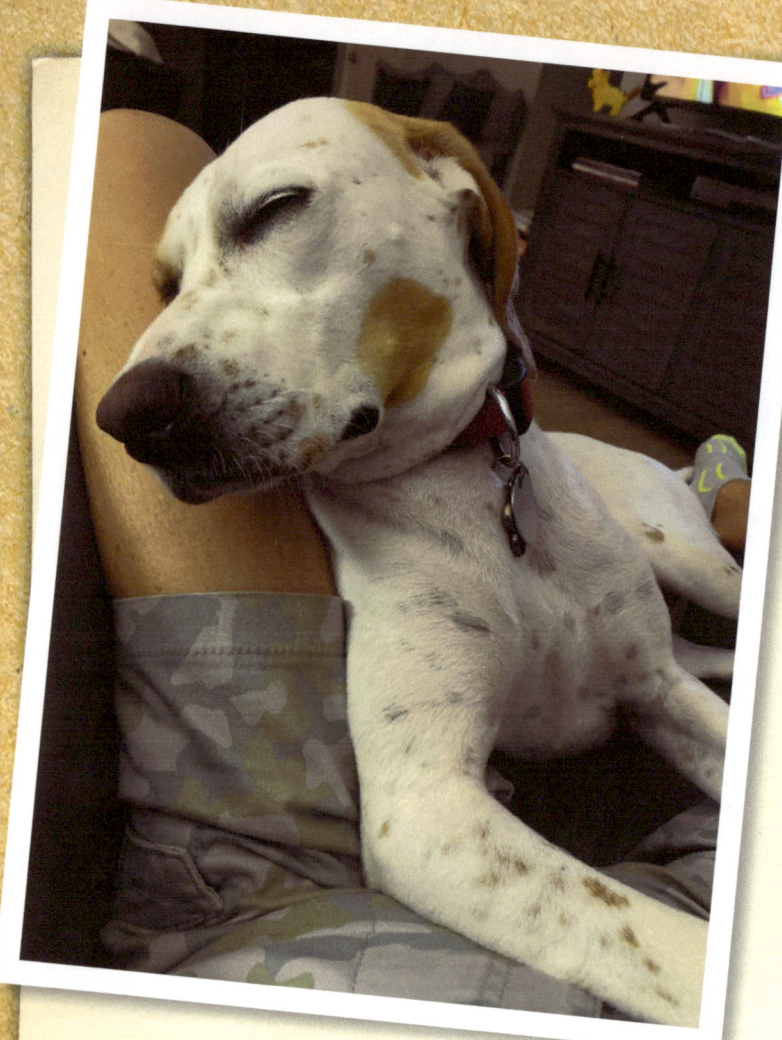

Mama waved goodbye to everyone as Dixie tugged on her leash.

They couldn't have asked for a more perfect day. When Mama and Dixie got home, they curled up together on their favorite chair. Dixie kissed Mama so much that it made her giggle.

Dixie the Rescue Dog had found her forever home with Mama, where she would never have to worry about returning to the animal shelter again. And now they both had new friends.

THE END

24

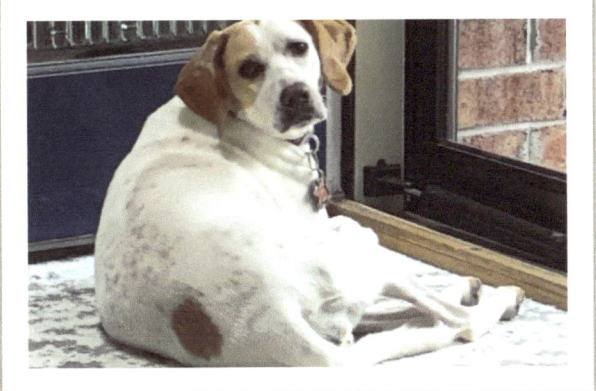 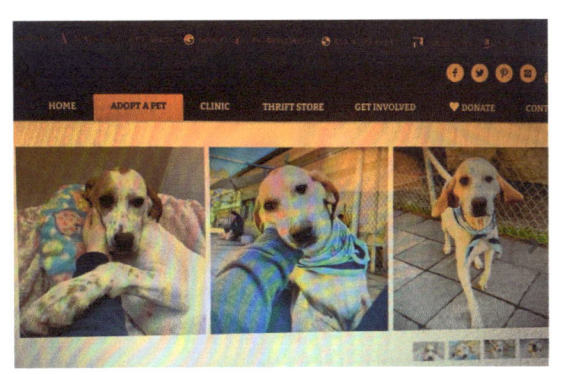 

Not all shelter dogs are as lucky as Dixie and her new friends were to find forever homes with loving families.

Countless others never get the chance to show how much joy they can bring to a family. Some are judged by their size, their color, and even the kind of dog they are. Some are puppies that need a lot of attention. Some are very old and just want to be loved. Some are mistreated or abandoned. Others, like Jarvis, are sick and need expensive medical care.

No matter why these lovable canines end up in a shelter, they all deserve families who will take good care of them and give them attention, and—most of all—love.

25

Dixie's Story

It took me quite a few years to overcome the heartbreak of losing my last dog, but I knew it was time to bring another special little girl into my life. I had just moved to the Lowcountry and didn't know anyone in the neighborhood. I felt very alone.

One Saturday evening, while scanning pictures of adoptable dogs at a local shelter, I came across this precious little girl. There was something about the look on her face. I had to meet her before someone else adopted her. It was Sunday morning, and I was so sure she would be the one for me that I bought water and food bowls, a comfy bed, some treats, and a bunch of toys. With a new leash in one hand and my heart in the other, I headed to the shelter first thing Monday morning.

The lady at the shelter introduced me to Dixie and told me she had been adopted twice before—and returned. I could only imagine why. Was she destructive or mean? Was she a biter? Or maybe she wasn't housebroken. I didn't know, but none of that seemed to matter— I decided to go with my gut. Dixie was coming home with me.

I could tell she'd already had some training and was housebroken. She didn't tear anything up except her toys—which was perfectly fine with me. I worked with her daily and didn't leave her alone for too many hours at a time. Still, I couldn't understand why she was returned to the shelter for a first time, let alone a second.

It's been over a year since Dixie became my forever baby girl. She is a heartfelt joy and a cherished constant companion. I wouldn't think of giving her up. She's an extraordinary dog whose boundless energy, limitless curiosity, and affectionate nature melt my heart. There's not a mean bone in her body. It turns out Dixie was the perfect dog for me. And I can't tell her enough times in a day just how much I love her.

Dixie was destined to be mine. I'm the lucky one.

Evie's Story

Evie is a happy, healthy 8-year-old Shih Tzu who loves dressing up, spa days, car travel, and going to the beach. She is very popular with her dog friends, but her life was not always so carefree.

Evie's first pet parent suffered a medical emergency and could no longer care for her. A concerned neighbor surrendered her to a shelter. Evie was seriously traumatized. She cowered, barked, and snapped at anyone who tried to touch her. One loving volunteer was able to earn her trust. They nurtured her back to health, comforted her, and tried to find her a new home.

Once Evie was medically cleared to be adopted, her new pet parent couldn't wait to meet her. At first, she sat shaking and shivering in her crate. She was afraid and uncertain about where she was going. It took about a month for her to adjust, but now she has a grassy yard to play in and pet parents who walk her every day.

Jack's Story

In 2016, Jack was rescued by an organization specializing in severely abused dogs. He was found wandering on the road and, at first, his rescuers thought he'd been hit by a car. He suffered from brain trauma and skull fractures, lost his right eye, and his ear canals had been destroyed–rendering him deaf. They rushed Jack to the emergency room, where luckily the doctors were able to save his life.

When his Dog-Mama saw his picture on Facebook, she adopted him on the spot. Since then, Jack has been enjoying a wonderful life with her. She loves him dearly and spoils him with all her heart. Jack is one lucky boy!

Lucy's Story

Lucy's new pet parents were sad when they moved away from family and friends. There was an animal shelter nearby where her Dog-Mama worked. Every morning the volunteers would walk the dogs right in front of her window. One day she noticed Lucy walking by, and she sensed in her heart that she would be the perfect companion.

It's been a couple of years since she was adopted. Lucy's made herself at home with her pet parents, where she has a big yard to play in, a warm, safe home, and all the love and attention she could ask for.

Pace's Story

Pace was born from a litter of sixteen puppies! Unfortunately, his original adoption failed and he was returned for readoption. When Pace's new family saw him, it was love at first sight. His rambunctious nature was just what their young son wanted. Through their love and patience, Pace overcame behavioral issues that may have stemmed from being part of such a large litter.

The fast-growing pup made himself right at home. He took to the water like a fish. His Dog-Mama would discover him swimming in the creek, tromping in the mud, then mindlessly tracking it into the house. As a seasoned adult, Pace lumbers around the neighborhood like King Tut, enjoying a carefree, happy, loving life with his adoptive family.

Jarvis' Story

Sometimes pets are in need of expensive medical care. That's what happened with Jarvis. Since his original pet parents couldn't afford the surgery he needed, they asked their veterinarian if she could find Jarvis a good home with someone who would be willing to adopt him given his condition and medical needs.

One look at Jarvis's pictures told his new mama he was the dog for her. She was willing to pay for his life-saving surgery and give him a loving forever home.

Penny Joy's Story

When her new owner first met Penny at the animal shelter, she weighed only 28 pounds. Penny was given her name because of her bright copper-colored coat.

Her new Dog-Mama noticed her romping around and joyfully playing with the other dogs. She was chasing her sister Lolita when Penny suddenly turned and came racing toward her, stopped and stared at the woman before giving her a wet kiss, then ran off to play. Her new Dog-Mama knew that Penny was destined to be hers.

Ten years later, Penny Joy is still happily living with her Dog-Mama in her forever home.

Maverick's Story

Sometimes fate is the great giver to a growing family. Maverick's new family was on their way home from a road trip when they decided to stop by a local shelter to check out the dogs. Having never owned a dog, the family wasn't planning to get one that day.

As they walked by Maverick's pen, he tilted his head to the side and gave them "the look"—the one that melts your heart. The family couldn't resist. They were hooked, and Maverick went home with them that very day.

Brinkley's Story

As a mere pup, Brinkley was adopted from a shelter in Georgia. The lucky pet-loving couple didn't have any idea this mixed-breed character would be so popular in the neighborhood. "Brinkley is very friendly and super handsome, or so everyone tells him!" says his Dog-Mama.

Brinkley loves attention from humans, especially when it comes in the form of a treat. He's a big old teddy bear who thrives on love and attention.

As the unofficial Mayor of the neighborhood rescue dogs, Brinkley stays busy welcoming everyone.

Baloo's Story

Baloo is Brinkley's older brother. He's eight years old now but was adopted from a shelter in South Carolina when he was three months old.

Baloo enjoys going on walks with his pet parents, but tires out a little faster than his younger brother Brinkley.

When he's not searching for lizards, Baloo usually snuggles up on top of a pile of pillows or one of his many comfy dog beds.

Oakley's Story

Oakley Cleetus is a pit-lab mix who found his "furever" family when his previous owner passed away. At first, they only intended to foster Oakley, then quickly fell in love with him. He needed an abundance of love and attention.

When his new pet parents adopted him, he was nothing but skin and bones. Some of his teeth were missing, and he was losing his hair.

He's now part of an active military family. He's well-traveled and loves meeting new people and animals wherever he goes. Oakley is a big snuggly bear who loves treats, going to the beach, and on car rides.

Oakley's pet parents think he's the best dog ever.

Nikki's Story

Nikki was five years old when she was adopted from a shelter in Georgia. Apparently, her former owner ignored her and left her in her crate for long periods of time. Her teeth were worn down from chewing on the metal in an attempt to escape. People at the shelter told her new pet parents not to crate her, so they never did. She happily has free run in the house.

It took a while for her pet parents to gain her trust, but with love and attention, regular walks, and treats, Nikki bounced back stronger than ever. Even though she's getting older and has a little trouble keeping up with her brother Scooter, going on walks is her favorite activity.

Scooter's Story

Nikki and Scooter are the best of buddies. Nikki's pet parents wanted her to have a dog brother, so a few years after adopting Nikki, they made another trip to the shelter and found Scooter. After Hurricane Irma, he was found running loose in a nearby town. The shelter tried for weeks to find his owner—without luck.

That's when this spunky little fellow caught the attention of his new pet parents. They thought Scooter would be the perfect companion for Nikki. He fit right into the family.

He has a lively personality and will chase anything that moves—squirrels, lizards, frogs, and even birds. He loves his toys, his best friend, and his loving family. Lucky dog and lucky pet parents!

A message for adults

If your family is considering adding a pet to your life, please support local no-kill shelters by adopting an animal already in need of a good home.

- If you can't have a pet of your own, ask how you can be of service to a shelter by volunteering, sponsoring an event or fundraiser, donating items needed, or by giving good old-fashioned cash.

- Educate yourself. Watch "Redemption: The No-Kill Revolution in America" at *https://www.nokilladvocacycenter.org*

When a person and a dog connect, it's magical.

Their age, color, breed, or illness doesn't matter. It's about compassion, caring, loyalty, and companionship.

Sheree's Story

As a young girl, Sheree started writing journals and poetry. Her career in advertising began when she worked for a local newspaper, then as an account supervisor and, subsequently, as the head of an advertising firm, where she won recognition for excellence as a writer and producer. After more than a decade of writing for television, radio, and print advertising, Sheree continued her love of writing by publishing her first three books—all of which were of different genres.

In keeping with her insatiability for variety, *Dixie the Rescue Dog Makes New Friends* is Sheree's first entry into writing children's books. It is with a clear purpose that she is dedicating a significant portion of the fruits of this effort to support "no-kill" animal shelters and advocacy programs nationwide.

Sheree volunteers her time and talents at The Pat Conroy Literary Center and is a member of the South Carolina Writer's Association and the Society of Children's Book Writers and Illustrators. She resides in the Lowcountry with her sweet companion, Dixie.